For Margery
on your graduation
Congratulations!
love-
Diana

Simple, mischievously clever and humorously insightful, A Short C₀
in Creating. . . *is one of those very rare treats which is at once of prof₀*
value and consistently entertaining.

Using a delightful array of charming illustrations, Robert Fritz has
ceeded in bringing a new level of vitality and sheer enjoyment to much o₁
pioneering and revolutionary work in the field of human creativity. In fa₀
Short Course in Creating. . . *is actually a practical guide or primer to crea₁*
the life you want, whatever your starting point or background may be.

From the very first page you'll be gently guided into a world popula
with endearing and often familiar characters interacting in situations you w
almost certainly recognize, animated by Fritz's unique imagination and p₀
etrating wit.

I invite you to experiment with Fritz's principles yourself. What can happ₀
is real and lasting change in your life.

Enjoy!

Robert Han

A short course in

Creating what you always wanted to

but couldn't before

because nobody ever told you how

because they didn't know

either.

A short course in

Creating what you always wanted to
but couldn't before
because nobody ever told you how
because they didn't know
either.

Illustrated by Robert Fritz and Mark Winter

by **DMA** *founder*

Robert Fritz

 DMA

Second Printing

Copyright © 1985 by Robert Fritz.

Manufactured in the United States of America.
Design and production by Stevan A. Baron, New York.
Typesetting by Crane Typesetting, W. Barnstable, Massachusetts.
Printed and bound by Maple-Vail Book Manufacturing,
Binghamton, New York.

DMA, Inc.   27 Congress Street   Salem, Massachusetts 01970

To Ivan, Tammy and Doug

1

2

LADIES AND GENTLEMEN, . . . THE LITTLE GUY

Hello, and thank you for reading. Today's subject is creating what you want in your life. First, we'll quickly cover the basic steps, and then we'll talk about how to use them.

Then we'll examine some actions people often take that lead . . . nowhere.

3

And finally, we'll discuss how to make creating what you truly want part of your everyday life.

4

AND NOW . . . SOME BASICS.

First,
know what
result you
want to
create.

Make sure it is
a final result .   .   .
not just a way
of getting the
result.

6

For example,
a result you want to create
might be a nice car that
runs all the time   .   .   .
or rather (hee hee) a car
that runs when you
want it to.

. . . So . . .
where was I? . . .
Oh yes.

First, make sure what you
want to create is a result . . .
not just steps along the way.

a car

Not a bank loan
designed to help you
buy the car.

Then . . . the result you want to create is a car.

mmm no

better

ah . . . that's it.

Any
questions?

Yes . . . when you are formulating
what you want, do you extrapolate from
existing data, or do you examine what the
situation seems to require, or do you
reach for meditative revelation while
attempting to evoke the deepest
desires, or do you attempt to select
the best from among the available
alternatives, or do you use a
simulated construct of a model of
causality, or do you research the
various possibilities and
parameters of implied science,
metaphysics and philosophy?

Nope . . .
I just make
it up.

. . . Once you know what you want . . . er . . . once you make up a result you want to create, the next thing you need to know is . . .

How to get there . . . right?

No, no . . . if you can do it . . . you know. "Is it possible?"

They're both wrong . . . You need to know why . . . Why do you want it . . . What are the reasons . . .

. . . As I was saying, once you know what you want to create . . . next you need to know <u>where you presently are</u>.

. . . For example, if you knew you wanted to go to Cincinnati, you would need to know where you were . . . what was your starting point.

. . . If you thought you were in Dubuque . . . but your starting point was actually in New York City . . . you might go southeast for 3 or 4 hundred miles . . . and you would end up in the Atlantic Ocean.

Of course . . . if you were in New York, and you thought you were in Dubuque, maybe you deserve to end up in the Atlantic Ocean.

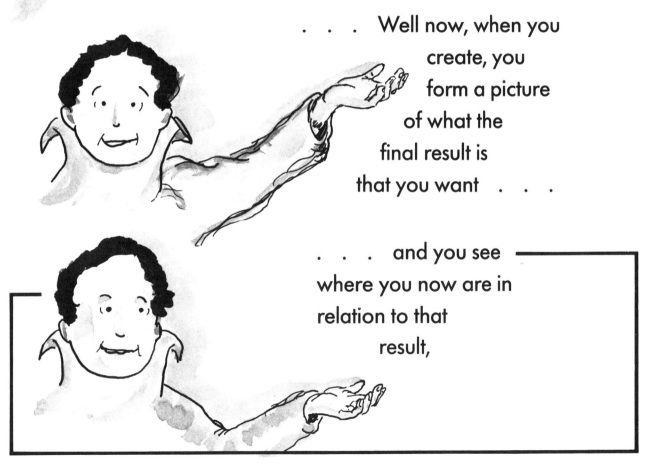

. . . Well now, when you create, you form a picture of what the final result is that you want . . .

. . . and you see where you now are in relation to that result,

15

What you want.

What you now have.

. . . and then you hold both at the same time.

We now get to a point that was personally revealed to me by Mother Nature herself . . . wise old girl that she is.

It is that

TENSION SEEKS RESOLUTION!

"SO WHAT?!" This is the key to my magical, mysterious and magnificent power . . . This is how I charm the gods . . . This is how I master the Muse . . . This is how the astronauts got to the moon . . . This is how Martina Navratilova won the championships . . . This is how birds fly and bees buzz . . . This is how Sinatra croons and Prince emotes . . . This is how flags wave and winds blow . . . This is how I go on like this without saying anything! (hee hee)

 . . . When you set out to create something, at first there will be a difference between what you *want* and what you *have*.

This difference creates a tension.

Now. What does this tension want to do?

Send out for tranquilizers.

Join a meditation group.

Get plenty of rest.

Sign up for psychotherapy.

Get into a relationship.

I'm not talking about emotional tension, but *structural tension* . . .

. . . Like, if I have a rubber band and I stretch it, there is a tension in the structure of the rubber band.

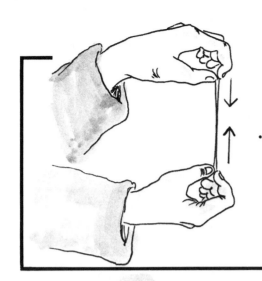

. . . and this tension
wants to resolve.

What will help you move
from where you are,
to where you want to be?

Setting it up so you
have the best chance
of accomplishing
what you want!

WORKING
WITH
THE
FORCES

When you know the result
you want to create, and
you also know where you
now are, you set up a
very useful tension. This tension is a
force and this force wants to *move*.

. . . So, as a creator, you stack the
cards in your favor by establishing
and holding tension.

Now, the tension can resolve
one of three ways.

By giving up what
you want.

By ignoring what
you now have.

Or by creating what you want.

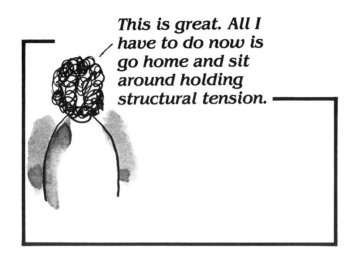

27

 . . . Ahem . . . Once you establish and hold structural tension, then action comes out of it.

You interest me, too.

 The actions you take may either <u>work</u> or <u>not work</u> in helping create the result.

If the actions work
you can continue taking
them . . . or discontinue
taking them.

Sometimes it is useful
to continue . . .

Sometimes it is useful
not to continue.

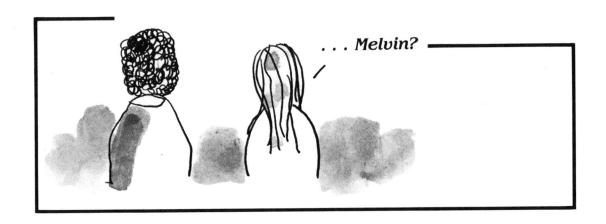

. . . *Melvin?*

You can
know what to
do by watching
the results.

 If the actions do not work you may either try the same thing . . .

Yes, Melvin.

Melvin?

. . . or try something new.

Well, my friends call me Lance.

In either case,
this is a learning
period . . .
. . . learning what
works and
what doesn't.

*My friends call
me Zelda, but
my real name
is Sue.*

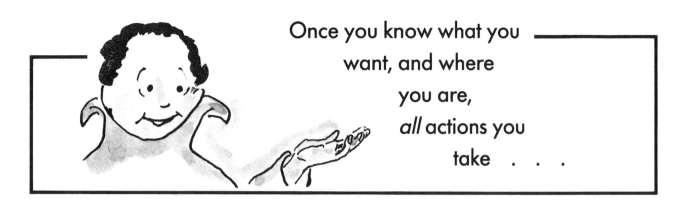

Once you know what you
want, and where
you are,
all actions you
take . . .

the actions that succeed . . .

Zelda is a nice name.

. . . and the actions that fail . . .

I never cared much for the name Lance or Melvin.

. . . help you create the final result.

I'll change my name if you'll have dinner with me.

It's a deal.

When you are creating, <u>Action</u> leads to final success, even when some of the actions fail.

But, on the other hand, <u>No Action</u> leads to final unwanted results . . . no change, or things getting worse.

ACTION: THE BIG THREE

There are three major types of actions people take:

1. **AVOIDANCE**

2. **OVERPOWERING**

3. **CREATING**

Most people learn to avoid what they
don't want when they are children.

It is good to avoid real danger. However, when avoidance becomes the major action in people's lives, they cannot move to where they *want* to go.

They can, at best, only avoid what they <u>don't</u> want.

Then avoidance becomes
like a strategy.
Here are the steps:

1. Find and focus on what
you want to avoid   .   .   .

2. Take action to avoid it.

I'll study as soon as this show is over.

But you forgot to turn the TV on.

What you want to avoid most often takes on an emotional characteristic such as . . .

guilt   fear   anger   sadness   resentment   pity

No one likes
to feel bad.

Everyone has had the
experience of taking actions
because they felt bad and
wanted to feel better.

. . . But some people notice the only time they
seem to act is when they are afraid
or mad or sad or resentful.

*Wake me when
I'm livid.*

These people develop a habit of trying to act by focusing on what makes them feel bad   .   .   .

The way this works is:

1. Establish a "clear picture" of what to avoid.

2. Make it worse than it is.

3. So you seem to have to force yourself into action.

Action based on avoidance has a
very limited ability to work,
short term   .   .   .

.   .   .   and cannot work
at all long term
because of how
avoidance works.

Focussing on "negative consequences"   .   .   .

leads to bad feelings   .   .   .

44

leads to action designed
to restore good feelings . . .

leads to less bad feelings . . .

leads to less action . . .

So if the avoidance actions
work they reduce the bad feelings . . .
leading to less reason to act.

Some people try to get others to
feel bad, so the others will take action . . .
like . . .

or . . .

Now, really get in touch with your anger! Think about all of those horrible things that have happened to you . . . like being born, for example!

or . . .

I don't care if you don't like Popeye . . . eat your spinach or I'll bop you one!

or . . .

THE GREEN CARROT HEALTH FOOD STORE

Oh no, they just discovered that cancer has been linked to people who worry about cancer.

I hope it was just in laboratory rats . . .

or . . .

PTA

and so . . . unless we do something about video games, our children will be doomed!! Do you hear me? Dooommed!!!

48

OVERPOWERING

Some people find, left to themselves, they do not take the actions they need to accomplish their long term goals.

So they use a strategy to overpower their inertia by trying to inspire themselves.

I can do it!
I can do it!
I can do it!
I can do it!
I can do it!
I can do it!
I can do it!
I can do it!

Eventually they run out of steam.

I can do it . . .
I . . . can . . . do it . . .
I can . . . . do . . . it
I . . . . . . can? . .
. . . do? . . . . it? . . .

When they run out of steam, they stop taking action.

The Form of this is:

Lethargy . . . .

Which leads to trying to generate action. ⎯⎯⎯⎯⎯⎯

Think positive!
Go for it!
You can have it All!
This is important!!
You can do it!
This is great!!
All right, Boy, this
time for sure!

Which leads to action.

Which leads to running out of steam.

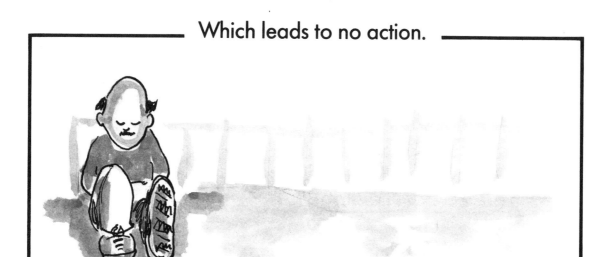

Which leads to no action.

Trying to overpower your lethargy . . . will not end up working.

Most people are lazy when they don't want to take actions they really don't care about.

This is natural.

AND NOW . . . THE KEY THAT CAN UNLOCK THE DOOR TO YOUR HIDDEN SELF

Both avoidance and overpowering rely heavily on your emotional state of being. After years of delving into the psyche of humankind as applied to human existence on this planet, I can now reveal the sum total of all of the work that has been done in the fields of psychology, sociology, psychiatry, theology, and aerodynamics
      (to mention just a few).

SOMETIMES YOU FEEL BAD

SOMETIMES YOU FEEL GOOD

SOMETIMES YOU FEEL DEGREES IN BETWEEN

When people feel bad, they often
try to stop feeling bad by
distracting themselves.

. . . BUT
PEOPLE DON'T LIKE TO
FEEL BAD . . .
SO . . .

Some people try to feel better by hiding what they truly want from themselves.

LOVE

HAPPINESS

MEANINGFUL WORK

FREEDOM

HEALTH

WHOLENESS

Other people hide what they do
have in their lives that they
don't like.

WORRY
BILLS
FIGHTS WITH
    LOVED ONES
SICK
BORED

Trying to stop the
bad feeling
is natural   .   .   .

But in order
to feel better   .   .   .

Feeling bad can be like heat . . . "the heat of the moment."

When you are in "the heat of the moment,"
it is often hard to recognize what
is in your own best interest.

Feeling bad is like a Short Term Demand.

I demand you do something!
. . . QUICK!

For many people, Short Term Demands seem to have all the power in their lives.

SHORT TERM DEMANDS

Oh no. I'll do whatever you say.

Maybe I should have stayed in bed.

People often move from one Short Term Demand to another, and another . . .

For others, Short Term Demands do not hold the cards . . . they do.

Since sometimes you feel good,
and sometimes you feel bad,
on the way to creating your
Long Term Goal you will feel
both good and bad.

And now . . .
THE TRUTH
ABOUT
THE TRUTH

CREATING

. . . And so, what have you learned so far about creating?

Make up the result you want to create.

See where you now are.

Hold both as structural tension.

Avoidance and overpowering don't work.

When I take action to feel better, I don't.

Zelda and I are in love.

. . . Now, when you are either avoiding or overpowering, you have to misrepresent reality. You cannot clearly see where you now are because you must . . . must . . .

In avoidance you make things seem <u>worse</u> than they are . . .

. . . and in overpowering you make things seem <u>better</u> than they are.

<u>But</u>, when you are creating
the results you want   .   .   .
you tell yourself   .   .   .

.   .   .   An accurate account
of reality with all its
flaws and favors, all its
highs and lows and in betweens,
all its disappointments,
indifferences and joys   .   .   .
you simply tell yourself
the   .   .   .   truth.

When you report the truth to yourself
you strengthen structural tension, which
helps you mobilize energy you can
use in creating.

And when you feel good, or bad,
or degrees in between, that is
just part of <u>where you are now</u>,
not merely some Short Term Demand.

*If I'd known
that 20 years ago,
I wouldn't have
an ulcer.*

*If I'd known that
20 years ago,
I wouldn't have
married my
first husband.*

*If I'd known that 20
years ago, I would
be at least 3
years and several
minutes older.*

It is important to know the difference between Long Term Goals and Short Term Demands because they lead to very different places and have very different results.

Short Term Demands will __always__ seek action. Most of these actions do not help create your Long Term Goals. These actions are aimed only to help you feel better . . . and even then they don't help you feel better very long.

To stay in touch with your Long Term Goals:

What do I want?

Dr. Merryweather's office

What actions do I need to create that result?

BIOCHEMISTRY FOR SICK PEOPLE

When you stay in touch with your Long Term Goals, needed actions are easier to take.

That Higby sure has stamina.

30,621
30,622
30,623 . . .

"CHOICE IS THE GARLIC AND OREGANO OF LIFE'S SPAGHETTI SAUCE."

Marco Polo, February 6, 1319

When you create, you
make choices about what
you want.

Let's call these results that are
most important to you
<u>primary choices</u>.

Once you know what
your primary choices are,
you then make other
choices to help support
your primary choices;
let's call these
<u>secondary choices</u>.

If your primary choice
is to weigh 103 pounds,
and you now weigh 152 pounds,
a secondary choice might be,
perhaps, to eat less   .   .   .
maybe even go on a diet.

Now, for all of you who
have gone on diets, or quit
smoking, or begun exercise
programs again, and again,
and again only to fail,
this will help you   .   .   .

Know what your
primary choice is, not
just by trying to remember,
but by asking <u>now</u> if you want it.

The time to make a secondary
choice is when there are at least
two things you want. Usually, your
Short Term Demand and Long Term
Goal are different. But, the truth
is, you want them both . . .
How do you decide?

90

The answer is:

See what you want more.

Some people never decide what things they want more and what things they want less.

When you create what you want, you never experience giving up something else that you want, rather you experience moving <u>toward</u> what you <u>most</u> want.

So to review . . .   (I'll do this all in one breath . . .   Uhhh) you start by conceiving of what you want to create, you then see what you presently have, and you hold both as structural tension. This tension naturally seeks resolution, helping you to bring your vision into reality. As you move from where you are to where you want to be, you make strategic choices. You make secondary choices to support each primary choice.

Then Short Term Demands do not sidetrack you from your Long Term Goals. Step by step you create what you truly want, on the days you feel great, on the days you feel so-so, and even on the days you feel lousy.

(Uhhhh)

YOU CAN CREATE MUCH OF WHAT YOU REALLY WANT IN YOUR LIFE!

. . . BUT MOST PEOPLE HAVE NOT HAD MUCH EXPERIENCE CREATING.

Since they have had little experience, they are not very good at it to begin with.

Since they are not very good at first, they often conclude they *cannot* create what they really want . . .

. . . and so they stop even considering what they want, and only consider what they think they can have.

. . . if people applied the same approach to driving, most of us would still be riding in horse drawn buggies.

I don't believe what I'm seeing.

People learn to drive over time. The more they practice, the better they usually are . . .

The same is true of creating what you want. The more you practice, the better you will be able to create.

If you have had only a little experience creating what you want, probably you are not as good at creating as you would like to be.

That man has a talent for understatement.

And notwithstanding, he is not wholly without his points of interest.

Withstanding or notwithstanding.

So you may think you can't create what you really want to create, and you might not even try.
But if you keep at it, you will find you often actually can create what you want, and you get better and better at it all the time.

And so, my friends, every time you set out to create, whether you succeed or fail, you are gaining experience and learning more and more, developing your ability to create what you truly want in your life! Thank you for reading, and keep creating.

99